You're Something Special, Snoopy!

**Selected Cartoons from
THE UNSINKABLE CHARLIE BROWN, Vol. 2**

Charles M. Schulz

CORONET BOOKS
Hodder Fawcett, London

First published 1972 by Fawcett Publications Inc.,
New York

Coronet edition 1973
Tenth impression 1982

Printed in Great Britain for
Hodder Fawcett Ltd.,
Mill Road, Dunton Green, Sevenoaks, Kent
(Editorial Office, 47 Bedford Square,
London, WC1 3DP) by
Cox & Wyman Ltd, Reading

ISBN 0 340 17322 X

AHEM!

OH, COME NOW! IF YOU'RE TRYING TO TELL ME IT'S SUPPERTIME, YOU'RE WAY OFF!

I REFUSE TO CHASE A STICK THAT HASN'T BEEN PROPERLY SANDED AND POLISHED!

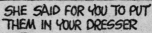

LOOK, THE FIRST OFFICIAL LEAF OF AUTUMN!

LEAVES HAVE BEEN FALLING FOR WEEKS... WHAT MAKES THAT ONE SO OFFICIAL?

I HAD IT NOTARIZED!

FANTASTIC!

HAVE YOU EVER KNOWN ANYONE WHO HAS THE GIFT OF PROPHECY?

JUST MYSELF

YOU?!

ABSOLUTELY! I CAN PREDICT WHAT ANY ADULT WILL ANSWER WHEN HE OR SHE IS ASKED A CERTAIN QUESTION..

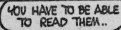

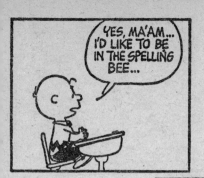

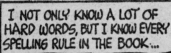

YES, MA'AM? ME? WHY DID I HAVE MY HEAD ON MY DESK? YOU DON'T KNOW? YOU'RE ASKING ME WHY I HAD MY HEAD ON MY DESK?

BECAUSE I BLEW THE STUPID SPELLING BEE, THAT'S WHY!!!

OH, GOOD GRIEF! NOW, I'VE DONE IT!

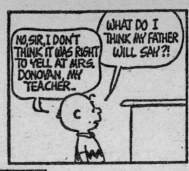

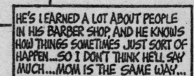

HELLO, SCHROEDER? GUESS WHAT...
I CALLED TO TELL YOU I'VE BEEN
LISTENING TO SOME BEETHOVEN MUSIC

I'VE ALSO BEEN READING HIS
BIOGRAPHY...IT'S VERY INTERESTING..
SORT OF SAD, AND YET SORT OF
INSPIRING...YOU KNOW WHAT I MEAN?

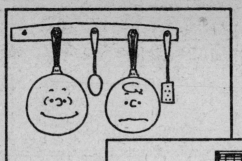

WHAT IF YOU AND I GOT MARRIED SOMEDAY, SCHROEDER?

AND WHAT IF WE WERE SO POOR YOU HAD TO SELL YOUR PIANO SO WE COULD BUY SAUCEPANS?

YOU KNOW WHAT?

I ALWAYS ENJOY SPECULATING ON WHAT OUR LIFE WOULD BE LIKE IF YOU AND I EVER GOT MARRIED, SCHROEDER...

I'LL BET WE'D HAVE A SON..AND HE'D PROBABLY BE A GREAT MUSICIAN JUST LIKE YOU...

IF DECEMBER TWELFTH IS HERE, CAN BEETHOVEN'S BIRTHDAY BE FAR AWAY?

GUESS WHAT...BEETHOVEN'S BIRTHDAY IS THIS WEEK, ISN'T IT? WELL, I'M GOING TO BAKE A CAKE, AND HAVE EVERYONE OVER! HOW ABOUT THAT?

I THINK SUCH AN EFFORT ON MY PART DESERVES A REWARD, DON'T YOU? LIKE MAYBE A LITTLE KISS...

I MEAN, AFTER ALL, SOMEONE LIKE YOURSELF WHO ADMIRES BEETHOVEN SO MUCH SHOULD BE WILLING TO REWARD A PERSON WHO WORKS HARD TO...

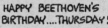

I'D GIVE ANYTHING TO BE ABLE TO TALK WITH THAT LITTLE RED-HAIRED GIRL...

THE AMAZING THING IS THAT I KNOW I'M THE SORT OF PERSON SHE'D LIKE! I MEAN I'M NOT ROUGH OR CRUDE OR ANYTHING

I'M NOT THE GREATEST PERSON WHO EVER LIVED, OF COURSE, BUT AFTER ALL, WHO IS? I'M JUST A NICE SORT OF GUY WHO....

..WHO NEVER GETS TO MEET LITTLE RED-HAIRED GIRLS!

HELLO, HARDWARE STORE? DO YOU HAVE ANY MINI-BIKES?

HOW MUCH MONEY IS A MINI-BIKE? I SEE...WELL, DO YOU HAVE MANY MINI-BIKES?

HOW MANY MINI-BIKES DO YOU HAVE? YOU DON'T HAVE MANY MINI-BIKES? HOW MANY?

THANK YOU FOR THE INFORMATION ON YOUR MINI-BIKES...NO, I DON'T THINK SO...I DON'T HAVE ANY MONEY FOR A MINI-BIKE...

HEY!

ZIP!

WHAT DO YOU THINK YOU'RE DOING?

NO FUTURE HUSBAND OF MINE IS GOING TO SIT AROUND HOLDING A BLANKET!

I'M NOT YOUR FUTURE HUSBAND! GIVE ME THAT BLANKET!

NO!

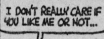

© 1970 United Feature Syndicate, Inc.

Wherever Paperbacks Are Sold

☐	04491 8	Good Ol' Snoopy (3)	75p
☐	04295 8	Here Comes Snoopy (6)	85p
☐	04405 5	All This And Snoopy Too (11)	75p
☐	12786 4	We Love You Snoopy (19)	75p
☐	12520 9	Charlie Brown And Snoopy (25)	75p
☐	15929 8	It's For You, Snoopy (28)	75p
☐	15698 8	You're Not For Real, Snoopy (30)	75p
☐	15696 1	You're A Pal Snoopy (31)	75p
☐	17322 X	You're Something Special Snoopy (33)	75p
☐	18303 9	There's No-One Like You Snoopy (37)	85p
☐	18663 1	Your Choice Snoopy (38)	75p
☐	19550 9	You've Got It Made, Snoopy (40)	75p
☐	19927 X	You're So Smart Snoopy (42)	75p
☐	20491 5	You're On Your Own Snoopy (43)	75p
☐	21236 5	It's All Yours Snoopy (45)	75p
☐	21983 1	You've Got To Be You, Snoopy (47)	75p
☐	22159 3	You've Come A Long Way, Snoopy (48)	75p
☐	22304 9	That's Life Snoopy (49)	75p
☐	22778 8	It's Your Turn, Snoopy (50)	75p
☐	22951 9	Play Ball, Snoopy (51)	75p
☐	24270 1	You've Got To Be Kidding Snoopy (54)	75p
☐	24517 4	It's Show Time Snoopy (55)	85p
☐	25478 5	Think Thinner Snoopy (58)	75p

All these books are available at your local bookshop or newsagent, or can be ordered direct from the publisher. Just tick the titles you want and fill in the form below.

Prices and availability subject to change without notice.

CORONET BOOKS, P.O. Box 11, Falmouth, Cornwall.

Please send cheque or postal order, and allow the following for postage and packing:

U.K. – 40p for one book, plus 18p for the second book, and 13p for each additional book ordered up to a £1.49 maximum.

B.F.P.O. and EIRE – 40p for the first book, plus 18p for the second book, and 13p per copy for the next 7 books, 7p per book thereafter.

OTHER OVERSEAS CUSTOMERS – 60p for the first book, plus 18p per copy for each additional book.

Name ....

Address...

....